KU-106-087

FONTANA

POCKET LIBRARY OF GREAT ART

Plate 1. SELF-PORTRAIT (*detail of color plate 29*)

DIEGO

VELAZQUEZ

(1599–1660)

text by

MARGARETTA SALINGER

Department of Paintings

The Metropolitan Museum of Art, New York

COLLINS

Fontana Pocket Library of Great Art

On the cover

THE INFANTA MARGARITA TERESA

(detail of colour plate 32)

Published in co-operation with Harry Abrams, N.V., Amsterdam, Holland, 1956

Plate 2. STILL LIFE: EGGS AND FISH (*detail of plate 4*)

The assertion that Velazquez is the most Spanish of painters and that his works manifest the qualities most typical of the Spanish temper may evoke a lively protest. Where, it will be asked, is the hot, unbridled passion of Carmen? where the abandoned gaiety of Goya's young dancing country folk? and where the fervent Christian mysticism of El Greco? But the statement may be maintained; for each of these allegedly Iberian characteristics, Velazquez presents other qualities equally, or even more typically, Spanish. Instead of passion, his works show control and disciplined restraint, courtesy, and considerate grace; for the gaiety of the eighteenth-century Goya, he offers the decorum and rigid etiquette of the most formal court in all Europe, and in place of the religious excitement and other-worldliness of El Greco's flamelike forms, he provides an unparalleled example of the sober realism that informs the art, the people, and the thinking of the entire peninsula. And in all the paintings of Velazquez, as in every allusion to himself, there are always dignity and pride.

For some reason, in Spain more than elsewhere, the artist and his works seem so inseparable that they must always be considered jointly. The bacchanals, the mythological paintings, the portraits of Charles V do not betray the kind of person Titian must have been. Nor do Michelangelo's Sistine ceiling and Medici tombs reveal anything except the huge stature of the morose giant who designed them. But to be Spanish is so vitally to be something in particular, to have so distinct and firm a core, that the paintings and the character of the man who made them are inextricably one. Velazquez left no journals, we have no great volume of his correspondence, no long series of revealing self-portraits; yet we come away from a careful examination of his works with a strong conviction of the manner of man he was: proud, noble, elegant, exquisitely refined and sensitive, gentle, serious, and brilliantly intelligent—intensely Spanish.

The writings of his teacher and father-in-law, the garrulous but probably trustworthy Pacheco, tell us a good deal about the early life of Velazquez; his later career as court painter and functionary in Madrid is illuminated by many documents and records. Especially informative is the material that he and famous contemporaries provided in 1658 as evidence of his worthiness to become a Knight of Santiago. He was born in Seville and baptized there on

Plate 3. THE VENERABLE MOTHER JERONIMA DE LA FUENTE
1620. 63 x 43¼". The Prado, Madrid

Plate 4. CHRIST IN THE HOUSE OF MARY AND MARTHA. *About 1619*

23¼ x 40⅛". The National Gallery, London

June 6, 1599. His full name was Diego Rodriguez de Silva y Velazquez, but he generally styled himself Velazquez (or Velasquez), the surname of his mother Jeronima, who was a well-born Sevillian. His father, Juan Rodriguez de Silva, came from a Portuguese family of the city of Porto and had good connections. This aristocratic if not noble parentage was a matter of considerable pride to him throughout his life. Along with his personal worth, it probably accounts for the important posts he held at court, and explains the urgency with which he struggled for nearly two years to establish his fitness for the knighthood that the King had offered him. The order was finally awarded the year before he died.

In 1610 Velazquez began a six-year apprenticeship with the foremost teacher of painting in Seville, Francisco Pacheco. Pacheco, who was advisor to the Inquisition on matters of art, painted tight, arid, but carefully composed portraits and religious pictures that strictly followed the conventions and rules he laid down in his book on the art of painting. He appears to have been a very good teacher, and according to his account and to Velazquez' earliest extant pictures, his young charge was rigorously and carefully trained. But from the start of his career, even when clinging closely to Pacheco's iconography and composition, Velazquez demonstrated his own talent and independence. After the end of his apprenticeship, when he had become a free master and had joined the Guild of St. Luke, Velazquez was married to Pacheco's daughter Juana.

He continued to live in Seville until 1623. In those years it was a rich and flourishing cosmopolitan city, a seaport into which poured exotic merchandise from many lands. Italian pictures certainly came there too, and Velazquez must have learned much outside the studio of old Pacheco. Most of the paintings that are now believed to have been done in the years before he went to

Plate 5. THE POET LUIS DE GONGORA. *1622*
20⅛ x 16⅛". Museum of Fine Arts, Boston

settle in Madrid are genre scenes, representations of everyday people going about their daily occupations in kitchens or taverns; they are painted very naturalistically, with strong lighting that recalls Caravaggio. Some, like *Christ in the House of Mary and Martha* (plate 4) have religious subjects buried in a corner, but religious paintings were never a specialty with Velazquez, and except for *The Coronation of the Virgin* (plate 18), the few there are were made before he was thirty-five.

If Velazquez had a premonition of future greatness, destiny did not require him to be patient very long. In the spring of 1622 he made a trip to Madrid to see the famous paintings there and at the Escorial. While in Madrid he painted a portrait of the poet Gongora (plate 5) and attracted the attention of important people. A year later he was called back at the command of the Count-Duke of Olivares, was given the opportunity to paint a portrait of the King, and in the fall of 1623 received the appointment of official court painter, with the proviso that he alone should portray Philip IV. From this time begins the magnificent series of portraits of the King and his household, which today, with the rest of the Hapsburg collections, are for the most part in the Prado in Madrid and the Kunsthistorisches Museum in Vienna.

The thirty-seven years of Velazquez' activity at court were punctuated by three events of great significance for his development: Rubens' visit to Madrid in 1628, and two voyages to Italy, the first in the years 1629–30, and the second from the end of 1648 until the middle of 1651. Rubens had already corresponded with Velazquez before his arrival in Spain, and while there—if we are to believe Pacheco's boast regarding his son-in-law—he had little to do with any other artist than Velazquez. Few episodes in the lives of famous men are as stimulating to the imagination as the excursion the two painters made to the Escorial—the young Velazquez, only five years in royal

Plate 6. DONA ANTONIA DE IPENARRIETA Y GALDOS AND SON
About 1631. 84⅝ x 43¼". The Prado, Madrid

employ, and the mature Rubens, famous over all Europe as artist and diplomat. How much we would give to know what they saw and what they said!

Velazquez' first voyage to Italy was a sightseeing trip, to Genoa, Venice, Rome, and Naples. The second was a royal mission, extended a good deal longer than King Philip wished, to bring back Italian pictures and sculptures for the royal collections.

The artist's final journey took place in the last months of his life, when he attended the King, not as painter, but as Chamberlain of the Palace, at the Isle of Pheasants, where the Infanta Maria Teresa was given in marriage to Louis XIV of France. On his return to Madrid at the beginning of summer he wrote in a letter to a friend that he was in good health, but on August 6, 1660, after a week of illness, Velazquez died.

For so long a career, it is an extremely small inheritance of pictures that he left us. One obvious explanation is the time he spent away from his studio discharging his duties as a household official. But this was not time entirely lost, for some of these duties must have afforded him opportunities for intimate observation of the lives of the King and his family, and gained him the insight into their characters which makes the portraits such accurate and penetrating estimates. Although his painting gives an impression of incredible speed of execution, the earnest process that preceded the translating of vision into actuality was probably a slow one. Over a period of forty years, he surely and steadily evolved an increasingly effective technique for the expression of his Spanish realism—ever more economical in statement and brush stroke, and always more masterful in his ability to seize the essential and fix it forever.

Plate 7. ST. ANTHONY THE ABBOT AND ST. PAUL THE HERMIT
About 1640. 101 7/8 x 74". The Prado, Madrid

Plate 8. CHRIST AND THE CHRISTIAN SOUL. *1629–31*
63⅜ x 80⅜". The National Gallery, London

COLOUR PLATES

PLATE 9

PHILIP IV

Painted about 1623–24. 78¾ x 40½"
The Metropolitan Museum of Art, New York
(Altman Collection)

Before his appointment to the royal service, Velazquez had painted a portrait of the King that met with universal approval from Philip and the court but is regrettably lost. This likeness was purchased by Dona Antonia de Ipenarrieta (see plate 6) and is mentioned in a receipt signed by Velazquez and dated December 4th, 1624. It is therefore the earliest of a long series in which we may trace the changes the years brought to the features and the bearing of King Philip. The full-length figure, clad in dark Spanish costume and standing beside a table, is a dignified formula Velazquez used in other early portraits—of the King, of his short-lived brother the Infante Carlos, and of the Count-Duke of Olivares. The gold chain with the Order of the Golden Fleece, and the fine white goods of the cuffs and the *golilla,* or stiffened collar, are the only distractions from the interest concentrated on the palely glowing skin of the King's hands and face.

PLATE 10

CHRIST AND THE PILGRIMS AT EMMAUS

Painted about 1625-26. 48½ x 52¼"
The Metropolitan Museum of Art, New York

The religious subject is here the main motif of the picture, not a subsidiary of a genre scene. A strong super-natural light strikes the head of Christ and illumines his wounded hand which rests on the shining white cloth as he is about to make the revealing gesture of breaking the bread. The heads of the two astounded pilgrims are lit by its subdued effulgence, but the palm and finger tips of the outstretched hand of the nearer man catch some of the glow, as if his wakening recognition of the Lord admits him to the glory.

Velazquez probably painted this picture soon after settling in Madrid, for though the baroque interest in dramatic lighting had been a characteristic of his Sevillian pictures, the type of Christ demonstrates a new effort toward idealization, and the color is higher in key. The head of the pilgrim facing the spectator is remarkably similar in type to the frontal hatless man in *The Topers* (plates 15 and 16), painted about 1628.

PLATE 11

PRINCE BALTASAR CARLOS ON HIS PONY

Painted about 1634. 82½ x 68½"
The Prado, Madrid

Baltasar Carlos, heir to the throne of Spain, was born in the autumn of 1629, not longer after Velazquez set sail for his first trip to Italy. The King waited for his favorite painter's return to order the first portrait of the little boy—very probably the one in the Museum of Fine Arts at Boston (plate 33), which shows him with his dwarf when the prince was one year and four months old. The equestrian portrait in the Prado, painted when he was five or six, was intended for a place high over a door, and the artist carefully calculated his effect with regard to the spectator's eye level. The soft hair and the defenseless appeal of the prince's baby features are pathetically at variance with his erect military bearing, his trained horsemanship, the rich costume and the royal baton. The limpid beauty of the color and the breath-taking freedom of the paint proclaim that Velazquez' art, quickened by the experiences of his Italian voyage, has now reached its full maturity.

Plate 12. APOLLO AT THE FORGE OF VULCAN

(commentary follows color plate section)

PLATE 13

PRINCE BALTASAR CARLOS IN HUNTING DRESS

Painted 1635-36. 75¼ x 40½"
The Prado, Madrid

This picture of the prince was probably painted shortly after the portrait on horseback; the features have crystallized, and the steady gaze directed at the spectator is that of a slightly older child. All of Velazquez' portraits of children magically combine dignity with tenderness. In the great Velazquez Salon of the Prado, this painting of the prince takes its place alongside similarly composed portraits of his father and uncle in hunting dress with no lessening of impressiveness. The picture was originally wider at the right, where only the breast and muzzle of a second hunting dog may be seen today. The arquebus that the prince holds is one that his father had received as a gift when he was a child.

Baltasar Carlos died at Saragossa in 1646, when he was seventeen, only a few months after it had been announced that he was to marry his father's niece, Mariana of Austria. Philip himself, widowed since 1644, married her in 1649.

PLATE 14
THE COUNT-DUKE OF OLIVARES ON HORSEBACK

(Detail of plate 36)
Painted after 1638. 123½ x 94⅜"
The Prado, Madrid

There is good reason to believe that the battle scene in the background (see entire picture, plate 36), behind the hoofs of the Count-Duke's dramatically rearing horse, commemorates the victory of 1638 against the French siege at Fuentarrabia. Olivares, who had been chief minister from the time of Philip IV's accession in 1620, was not a military man nor was he actually present at the battle. The triumph, however, was laid to strategy he had planned, and he received the title of General of Fuentarrabia to add to the other distinctions with which the King had honored him.

Don Gaspar de Guzman, Count-Duke of Olivares, was born in Rome when his father was ambassador there, and lived much in Seville, where his house was a meeting place for poets and scholars. It was he who had called the attention of Philip to the young Velazquez, who in 1624 painted a full-length, standing portrait of Olivares. He was banished from court in 1643 and died two years later.

LIFT FOLD FOR ENTIRE PAINTING –
DETAIL AT RIGHT

PLATES 15 & 16

THE TOPERS (THE TRIUMPH OF BACCHUS)

Painted 1628-29. 64⅞ x 88¾"
The Prado, Madrid

This painting is at the same time Velazquez' first ambitious picture with many figures and his last important work before he left Spain in the late summer of 1629 for his first trip to Italy. It still looks backward to his early works done in Seville, for of the nine figures only two, Bacchus himself and the youth reclining beside him, are the nudes that we expect to find in bacchanals. The rest are lusty countrymen, roughly clothed in contemporary dress and exhibiting the same unposed air that charterized the naturalistic genre scenes which the Spanish call *bodegones*. But *The Topers* differs sharply from these: the genre scenes sought and achieved an effect of a casually chosen slice of life, whereas *The Topers* is carefully composed around the light flesh of Bacchus in the center; and the figures, arranged within a given space, move backward and forward in depth.

PLATE 17

AESOP

Painted about 1639-40. 70½ x 37"
The Prado, Madrid

This picture of the Greek philosopher is said to have been made for the Torre de la Parada, the royal hunting lodge for which Rubens painted some of the greatest of his late works. There is a vivid contrast between this imaginary likeness and Velazquez' official court portraits, where convention is observed even in the dress of the baby Infantes, who bear themselves with royal dignity. Aesop's heavy figure, slumping carelessly, is wrapped in a clumsy, shabby robe, negligently fastened about the waist with a light-colored sash. All this indifference to externals seems like a carefully planned foil for the serious, enigmatic expression of the rugged head, tilted a little to one side with an appraising look. Velazquez' rapid, certain brush strokes construct a rough thatch of hair, model the rocklike bones of cheek and brow and chin, and fleck with high light and shadow the firm, silent mouth.

ÆSOPVS

PLATE 18

THE CORONATION OF THE VIRGIN

Painted about 1641. 69¼ x 48¾"
The Prado, Madrid

The Spanish philosopher Ortega y Gasset has written that Velazquez "never allows himself to be carried away by a myth beyond the confines of this world," but "asks himself what actual situation near at hand corresponds to the ideal situation of the theme of the myth." This analysis of the artist's attitude toward his mythological paintings might with equal justice be applied to his religious pictures. Extraordinarily alert to all the beauties of this world, and marvelously endowed with the power of re-creating them in paint, Velazquez conceived the scene in which the Virgin Mary receives from her divine Son and God the Father the final accolade of heavenly acceptance, much as if it were a solemn ceremony of the Spanish court—traditional, dignified, and symmetrically ordered. The picture, full of sweetness and peace emanating from the gravely beautiful types of childhood, maturity, and age, was painted for the oratory of Queen Isabelle, Philip's first wife.

Plate 19. THE SPINNERS *(detail of plate 39).*

Commentary follows color plate section

PLATE 20

PHILIP IV: THE FRAGA PORTRAIT

Painted 1644. 53 1/8 x 38 1/2"
The Frick Collection, New York

In 1644, Velazquez accompanied the King when he left Madrid to join his armies in Aragon. In the early summer at Fraga, in a crude makeshift studio that lacked door, window, and floor until royal order made good these deficiencies, he painted a portrait of the King that is unrivaled in its sheer glory of color and textures, and its inspired manipulation of paint. Perhaps some of its spell is due to tension and pressure, for documents record that the picture was painted in less than three full days. Philip, who in this single instance poses facing left instead of right, is dressed in a costume (minutely described by a seventeenth-century writer) that he wore to honor his soldiers. The "red woolen coat" with "trimming of massy silver braid" becomes at Velazquez' hands a strange subdued rose that borrows something metallic from the glint of the simulated silver threads of the embroidery, laid on with the most incredibly knowing and telling flash of brush.

LIFT FOLD FOR ENTIRE PAINTING —▶
DETAIL AT RIGHT

PLATES 21 & 22
THE SURRENDER OF BREDA (THE LANCES)

Finished by 1635. 121⅛ x 144¾"
The Prado, Madrid

Breda, which lies near the southern border of presentday Holland, was the scene of a great Spanish victory over the Netherlands in 1625. Velazquez painted this justly famous picture some time within the next ten years. The superb complex composition, which involves the grouping of two large crowds, the handling of many planes receding into deep space, and a richly varied twodimensional pattern, is the high point of his accomplishment in the years immediately after his influential voyage to Italy. But the adept marshaling of all these pictorial resources only underlines the focal point—the meeting between Justin of Nassau, who tenders the key of the city, and Ambrosio Spinola, whose gracious, kindly gesture makes him seem less a conqueror than a courteous guest. Velazquez had an opportunity to evaluate the quality of Spinola while traveling in the same ship with him in 1629. Rubens, who knew him well, described him as "a sure and safe man," "the wisest and most prudent person" he had ever met.

PLATE 23
THE BUFFOON DON SEBASTIAN DE MORRA

Painted about 1643-44. 41¾ x 31⅞"
The Prado, Madrid

The circumscribed life and conduct at court, the endless ceremonies, and the vacuum between ceremonies, must have induced unlimited tedium and boredom. The empty hours were mitigated somewhat with the medieval entertainment provided by a constantly shifting population of royal jesters, idiots, and dwarfs who apparently received the same sort of affectionate pampering as the various dogs that appear in so many of Velazquez' pictures. In portraying these people, the painter made a sharp distinction between the different sorts of abnormality. Sebastian de Morra and the buffoon known as "*El Primo*" (see plate 35) turn toward the spectator countenances that indicate, to be sure, a brooding emotional awareness of their plight, but not a total befogging of the mind itself. Indeed, *El Primo,* who is shown sitting on the ground surrounded by books and writing materials, was an assistant in one of the royal secretariats.

Morra was summoned in 1643 from Flanders, where he had belonged to the entourage of Philip's brother, to enter the service of Baltasar Carlos. He died in 1649. It is hard to fathom the meaning conveyed by the pitiful posture and the intent, dark, handsome eyes.

PLATE 24

FRANCISCO LEZCANO

Painted about 1638-42. 42 1/8 x 32 3/4"
The Prado, Madrid

Like Sebastian de Morra, Francisco Lezcano, who had come to court in 1634, was assigned to amuse Prince Baltasar Carlos. He died in 1649, about half a dozen years after this portrait was painted, having spent three of those years in banishment because he had invoked royal displeasure.

With wonderfully loose, easy brushwork Velazquez has depicted the sad creature perched on a rock in a vague mountain landscape, his beclouded brain symbolized by the blackness of the cliff against which his uncoordinated small body is posed. His lips are parted in a meaningless expression, and his head tips back, revealing misshapen nostrils and unfocused eyes, which are only dark blurs beneath his half-lowered lids. One wonders whether the presence at court of these miserable bits of humanity sometimes provided, along with entertainment, lessons in compassion.

PLATE 25

POPE INNOCENT X

Painted 1650. 55 1/8 x 47 1/4"
The Doria-Pamphili Gallery, Rome

Innocent X was seventy-six years old when the visiting Spaniard painted him in Rome in 1650, sitting squarely upright in his great armchair regarding posterity with cold vigor. Born Giovanni Battista Pamphili, he had become Pope in 1644 and held office almost eleven years. In his youth he was apostolic legate to Spain, and his papacy initiated a police favoring the Hapsburgs.

Velazquez here follows the Italian pattern for a papal portrait. He brought to the painting of this likeness not only his superlative observation of the minute traits that reveal character, but all the genius his brush commanded in his last period. The brilliant high lights and the lively shadows of the red cape equal in mastery the rich textures of the paint that depicts the finely pleated white vestment, the collar, and the sleeve.

LIFT FOLD FOR ENTIRE PAINTING
DETAIL AT RIGHT

PLATES 26 & 27
VENUS WITH THE MIRROR ("THE ROKEBY VENUS")

Painted before June, 1651. 48½ x 68⅞"
The National Gallery, London

More than two centuries before Renoir declared that black is the queen of colors, Velazquez had used it again and again—to set off royal dignity, the tenderness of childhood, and magnificently here to display the beauty of a woman's body. The silken drapery serves a double purpose: it not only contrasts with the infinitely variable tones of the flesh, but accents the undulating curves, and shimmering softly in its folds repeats in a lower, simplified key the complicated melodic line. Venus' pure loveliness is enhanced by the absence of the jewels with which Titian and Veronese adorned their nudes. Other paintings of Venus by Velasquez are recorded in old inventories, but lamentably lost. This one, long at Rokeby Hall in Yorkshire, was almost certainly painted for Philip IV, who followed his grandfather Philip II in his taste for mythological pictures celebrating the female nude. It once belonged to Goya's beloved Duchess of Alba.

ENTIRE PAINTING AT RIGHT
LIFT FOLD FOR DETAIL

PLATES 28 & 29

THE MAIDS OF HONOR ("LAS MENINAS")

Painted about 1656. 125½ x 108⅞"
The Prado, Madrid

When Velazquez painted this unrivaled picture of the maids of honor attending Princess Margarita Teresa while she poses for her portrait, he borrowed no traditional formula for the complicated arrangement of a group portrait with many figures. In his fifty-eighth year, at the peak of his powers, master of anything he chose to do, he conceived a richly varied, completely original composition. The enclosed area flows outward on all sides through doors and windows, into light and shadow, to suggest, without revealing, the adjoining space. We have the illusion of being privileged, unobserved observers in the studio. The painter himself (see plate 1) appears with brush and palette, pausing momentarily in his work on the huge canvas that shuts off our view on the left-hand side of the room. The King and Queen must be standing somewhere near our own vantage point, for a mirror on the rear wall reflects their images. A courtier in black, silhouetted against bright light, halts on a short flight of steps at the back. Painter and child, dwarfs and dog, all are arranged in credible, eternal relation.

PLATE 30

THE INFANTA MARIA TERESA

Painted about 1651. 50⅜ x 38½"
Kunsthistorisches Museum, Vienna

Maria Teresa, born in 1638, was the younger sister of Baltasar Carlos, and like him the child of Philip and his first wife, Isabella de Bourbon. Her mother died when she was six, and her new Austrian step-mother was only a few years older than she was. When Maria Teresa was twenty-two, she was wedded to Louis XIV, and received little admiration from the Frenchwomen at her husband's court, who were very scornful of her Spanish style of rouging and dressing. Here the grotesque exaggeration of her huge wig and widespreading stiffened skirt (called what in very truth it was, a *guardainfante*), serves to enhance the design and makes the custome the occasion for Velazquez' most aesthetically satisfying and subtle color and brushwork. In all his work there is no line more beautiful than the curve defining the overskirt, which diminishes and swells like a note of music, finally disappearing beneath the handkerchief.

PLATE 31

A GARDEN AT THE VILLA MEDICI, ROME

Painted 1649-50. 18⅞ x 16½"
The Prado, Madrid

When Velazquez was in Rome for the first time in 1630, he left his lodgings in the Vatican at the beginning of summer and went to stay for two months in the Villa Medici, where he could copy the numerous sculptures on the grounds and enjoy the air high above the city. For this reason, the two delightful landscapes in the Prado which show the grounds of the villa were long thought to have been painted at the time of this visit, works of his early maturity. Recently, however, scholars have agreed that the technique of the paintings makes it certain that they are souvenirs of his second visit to Rome. Always a realist, and always a portraitist, he gives us in the rich variety of the greens of cypresses and hedge, in the warm tones of the wall, a record of the very light and air that he experienced sensuously in that lovely spot.

PLATE 32

THE INFANTA MARGARITA TERESA

Painted about 1654. 50⅜ x 39⅜"
The Prado, Madrid

When Philip married again after Baltasar Carlos' death, hopes ran high that his young bride, Mariana of Austria, would give him another son. She did eventually produce the frail Felipe Prosper (see plate 42), who lived only four years, and finally the unattractive Charles II, who was to be the last of the Spanish Hapsburgs. This sturdy little girl, however, had been born in the early years of the marriage, in 1651. Velazquez painted her more than once, notably as the central figure of *The Maids of Honor* (plates 28 and 29). She was married at the age of fifteen to Emperor Leopold of Austria, and died in 1673. She was three when she posed for this portrait, which owes some of its direct charm to the fact that she was not yet grown up enough to be encased in the enormous formal farthingale. Its beauty is due even more to the fresh light color, the superbly painted flowers, and the painter's magical depiction of textures, especially the silky, bodiless blonde hair.

COMMENTARY FOR PLATE 12
APOLLO AT THE FORGE OF VULCAN

Painted 1630. 88⅛ x 114⅞"
The Prado, Madrid

An early biographer of Velazquez asserts that he painted this picture while he was in Rome in 1630. No peasants in contemporary dress here look out at the spectator, as in the earlier Bacchus picture (plate 15) and the Sevillian paintings. All the characters participate in the action, directing a unified gaze toward the classically idealized figure of Apollo, who enters the scene in a blaze of splendor at the left. He has come to warn Vulcan, the blacksmith unsuitably mated to Venus, that his wife is conducting a liaison with Mars. The expression of shock and wary incredulity on the honest face of the smith contrasts with the suave, sophisticated indifference in the Olympian profile of Apollo. The other smiths pause in their work to listen to the astonishing news with deep interest. The nude torso of Vulcan is beautifully modeled, and the still life of armor and blacksmith's fittings seems appropriate to the setting.

COMMENTARY FOR PLATES 19 AND 39

THE SPINNERS (THE FABLE OF ARACHNE)

Painted about 1657. 86⅞ x 110½"
The Prado, Madrid

In his early painting of *Christ in the House of Mary and Martha* (plate 4), Velazquez made his real subject an everyday kitchen scene, relegating the biblical story to the aperture behind. In this masterpiece of his last years, he similarly combined the activities of a tapestry manufactory with a dramatization, in the alcove at the back, of the classical fable of the weaver Arachne. The rear wall of the alcove is hung with a woven copy of Titian's painting of *The Rape of Europa,* one of the most celebrated of Jove's escapades. The helmeted figure gesturing angrily in the background at the left is Minerva, who jealously resented the skill and boastfulness of Arachne and in filial piety punished her for having woven a tapestry that jibed at the amours of Jove. The incomparable shoulder and outstretched arm of the barefoot girl in the foreground epitomize the art of Velazquez, who always found the visible world inexhaustibly interesting and beautiful.

Plate 33. PRINCE BALTASAR CARLOS WITH A DWARF. *1631*
55⅛ x 31⅞". Museum of Fine Arts, Boston

Plate 34. A LADY WITH A FAN. *About 1640*
36 1/8 x 26 3/4". The Wallace Collection, London

Plate 35. THE DWARF "EL PRIMO." *1644*
42⅛ x 32¼". The Prado, Madrid

Plate 36. THE COUNT-DUKE OF OLIVARES ON HORSEBACK
After 1638. 123½ x 94⅜". The Prado, Madrid

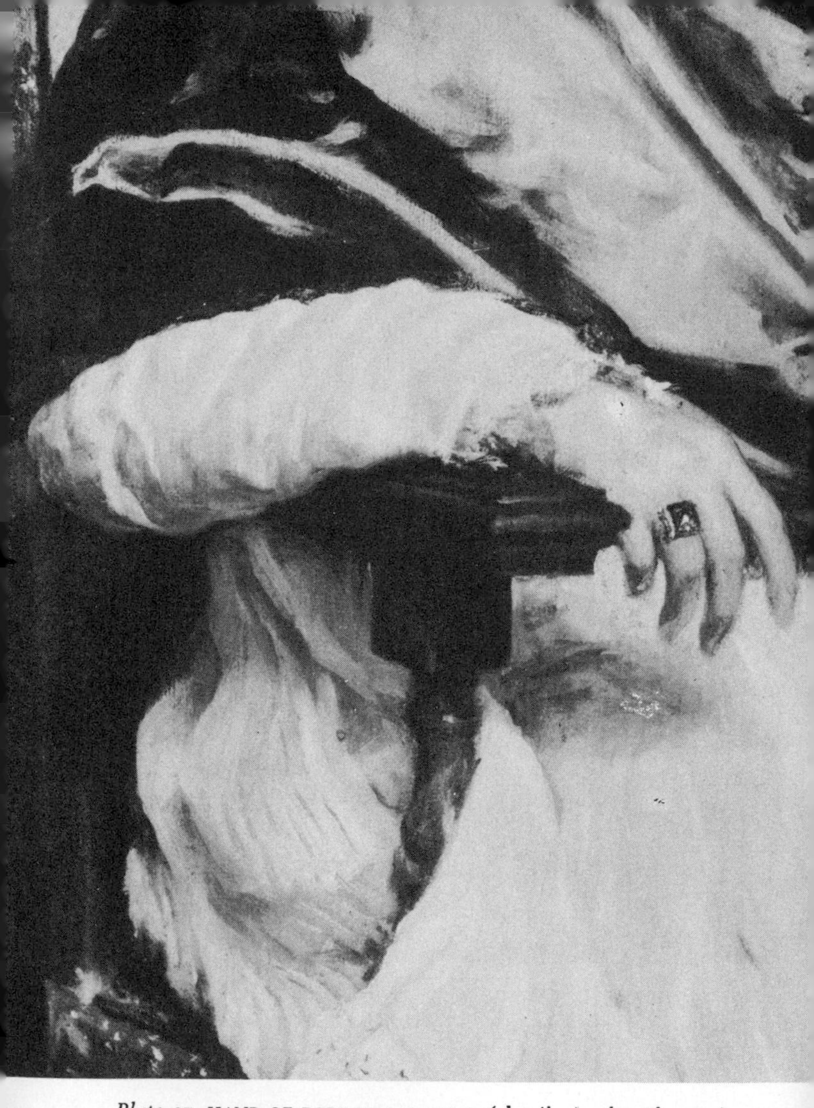

Plate 37. HAND OF POPE INNOCENT X (*detail of color plate 25*)

Plate 38. HEAD OF THE VIRGIN (*detail of color plate 18*)

Plate 39. THE SPINNERS

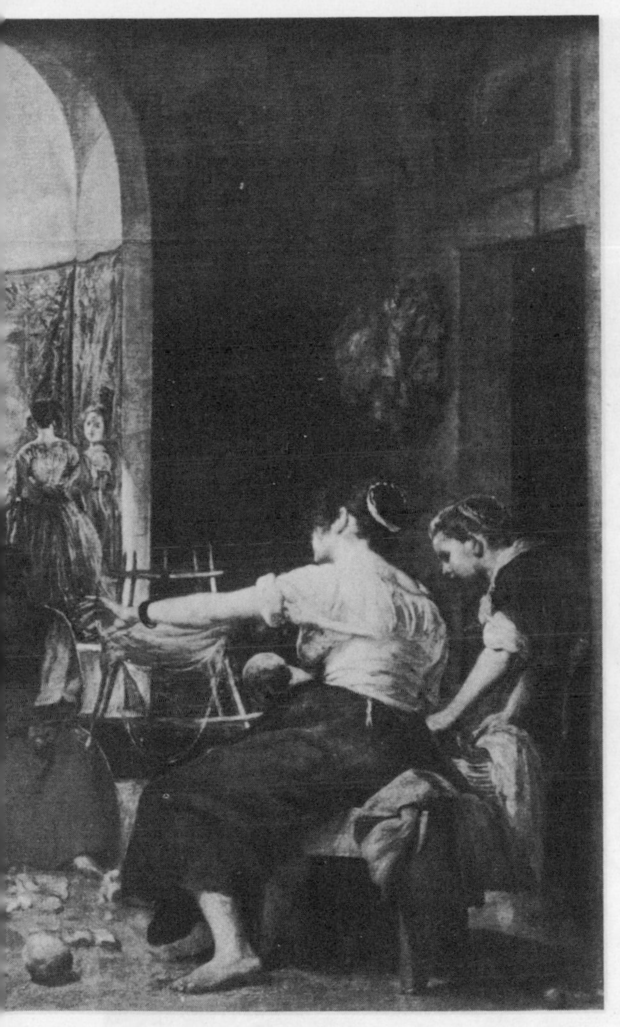

See plate 19 and commentary following color plate section

Plate 40. MARS. *About 1640*
70½ x 37⅜". The Prado, Madrid

Plate 41. MERCURY AND ARGUS. *About 1659. 50 x 97⅞". The Prado, Madrid*

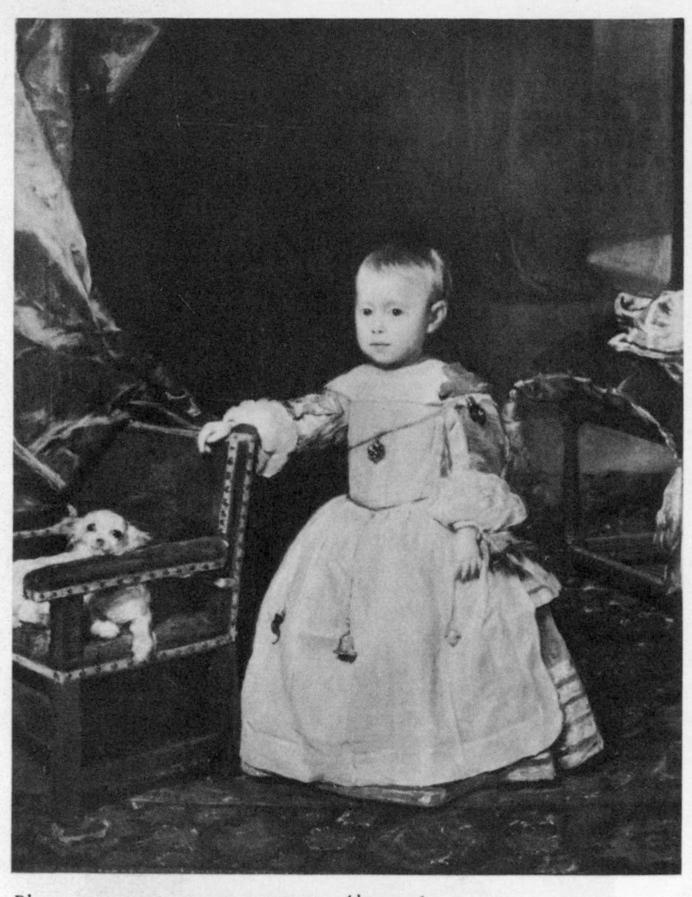

Plate 42. PRINCE FELIPE PROSPER. *About 1659*
50⅜ x 39". Kunsthistorisches Museum, Vienna

AT RIGHT: *Plate 43.* DOG AND CHAIR (*detail of plate 42*)

BIOGRAPHICAL NOTES

1599	Diego Velazquez (pronounced *vay*-LATH-*kayth*) baptized June 6 in Seville.
1610	Begins apprenticeship to Francisco Pacheco.
1617	Applies for admission to the painters' Guild of St. Luke in Seville.
1618	Marries Pacheco's daughter, Juana de Miranda.
1619	Finishes his first dated picture, *The Adoration of the Magi,* now in the Prado, Madrid.
1622	Makes his first trip to Madrid; paints the portrait of the poet Gongora (plate 5).
1623	Makes second trip to Madrid, summoned by Count-Duke of Olivares. Paints portrait of King Philip IV and on October 6 enters the King's service.
1629–31	First trip to Italy.
1644	Accompanies the King to Aragon; paints his portrait at Fraga (plate 20).
1648	Leaves Madrid in late fall for second trip to Italy; returns in June, 1651.
1660	Attends the ceremonies of Maria Teresa's marriage to Louis XIV on the Isle of Pheasants; dies on August 6.

VELAZQUEZ AND THE FRENCH IMPRESSIONISTS

It is hardly surprising that the French painters of the last century, especially Manet and Renoir, should have found the paintings of Velazquez so sympathetic and so admirable. Their enthusiasm indeed bears out the contention that Impressionism was not an isolated national movement in the history of painting but is a way of looking at the world, and of re-creating it with a minimum of descriptive brushwork. The Musée Espagnol, which had been formed by Louis Philippe and included nineteen works by or ascribed to Velazquez, was on exhibition at the Louvre from 1838 to 1848. Manet, at least, must have known it during his youth; Spanish subjects abound in his early works, painted before his visit to Spain in 1865. On his first Sunday morning there he wrote to Fantin an ecstatic letter: "Velazquez, in himself, is worth the trip! He is the painter of painters"; and one of the Prado paintings of a court fool he described as "perhaps the most astonishing piece of painting that has ever been done."

Some twenty years later, in 1881, Renoir also made a trip to Spain and was likewise enchanted. He found in Velazquez an "aristocratic quality" that delighted him, and "not the slighest shadow of sentimentality. . . . His work looks so easy, but think of the experimentation it must have taken. . . . He gives you thick and heavy embroideries with a simple rubbing of black and white. I know nothing more beautiful than *The Spinners*! The background of that picture is sheer gold and diamonds." And he "went back again and again" to look at *The Surrender of Breda,* declaring characteristically, "I almost felt like kissing those horses!"

With more restraint but with equal appreciation, Degas wrote from Madrid in 1889, "Nothing, absolutely nothing, can give an idea of Velazquez."

SOME OTHER BOOKS ABOUT VELAZQUEZ

Velazquez, Spanish School. London, Medici Society, 1950

H. DUMONT. *Velazquez.* London, Hyperion Press, 1950

E. LAFUENTE (Editor). *Velazquez.* London, G. Allen, 1945

JOSÉ ORTEGA Y GASSET. *Velazquez.* London, Collins, 1954

M. SALINGER. *Diego Velazquez* (1599–1660). London, Thames & Hudson, 1955

EDITORIAL NOTE

The object of this series is to introduce the great artists of the world to the general reader at a price and in a format suitable ot his pocket. The greatest pains have been taken to attain faithful reproduction of the true colour values of the paintings, but no mechanical process exists today which can do justice to the full beauty of the original works of art.
The publishers will feel rewarded if readers are persuaded to see the masterpieces themselves in the collections and galleries to which they are directed in the text.

PRINTED IN HOLLAND
OFFSET SMEETS WEERT